W9-BJO-994

WELCOME

A Unitarian Universalist Primer

WELCOME

A Unitarian Universalist Primer

Edited by Patricia Frevert

Skinner House Books

Boston

Printed in the United States

Cover design by Suzanne Morgan
Text design by Jeff Miller

ISBN 1-55896-544-0
978-1-55896-544-7

6 5 4 3 2 1
11 10 09 08

Library of Congress Cataloging-in-Publication Data

Welcome : a Unitarian Universalist primer / Patricia Frevert,
    editor.
      p. cm.
    Includes bibliographical references.
    ISBN-13: 978-1-55896-544-7 (pbk. : alk. paper)
    ISBN-10: 1-55896-544-0 (pbk. : alk. paper) 1. Unitarian
Universalist Association. 2. Unitarian Universalist Association—
Doctrines. I. Frevert, Patricia.

    BX9841.3.W44 2008
    230´.9132—dc22

                                                    2008019786

We gratefully acknowledge permission to reprint the words and music to "Spirit of Life" by Carolyn McDade © 1981 Carolyn McDade.

This small book welcomes you to Unitarian Universalism and tells you something about our faith. No piece of writing can capture how Unitarian Universalism is lived in the world: the congregations, the ministers, the community action, the music, the children. Nevertheless, we hope this will give you a taste of our worship, history, theology, and practice. The words on these pages are meant to open the door, and ask you in.

Contents

May the Love which overcomes all differences,
which heals all wounds,
which puts to flight all fears,
which reconciles all who are separated,
be in us and among us
now and always.

—FREDERICK E. GILLIS

What Do Unitarian Universalists Believe?

We believe in the freedom of religious expression. All individuals should be encouraged to develop their own personal theologies, and to present openly their religious opinions without fear of censure or reprisal.

We believe in the toleration of religious ideas. All religions, in every age and culture, possess not only intrinsic merit, but also potential value for those who have learned the art of listening.

We believe in the authority of reason and conscience. The ultimate arbiter in religion is not a church, nor a document, nor an official, but the personal choice and decision of the individual.

We believe in the never-ending search for Truth. If the mind and heart are truly free and open, the revelations that appear to the human spirit are infinitely numerous, eternally fruitful, and wondrously exciting.

We believe in the unity of experience. There is no fundamental conflict between faith and knowledge, religion and the world, the sacred and the secular, since they all have their source in the same reality.

We believe in the worth and dignity of each human being. All people on earth have an equal claim to life, liberty, and justice—and no idea, ideal, or philosophy is superior to a single human life.

We believe in the ethical application of religion. Good works are the natural product of a good faith, the evidence of an inner grace that finds completion in social and community involvement.

We believe in the motive force of love. The governing principle in human relationships is the principle of love, which always seeks the welfare of others and never seeks to hurt or destroy.

We believe in the necessity of the democratic process. Records are open to scrutiny, elections are open to members, and ideas are open to criticism—so that people might govern themselves.

We believe in the importance of a religious community. The validation of experience requires the confirmation of peers, who provide a critical platform along with a network of mutual support.

—DAVID O. RANKIN

The Seven Principles

Unitarian Universalism encompasses a wide range of beliefs. These seven principles sum up the core values that our congregations promise to affirm and promote.

- The inherent worth and dignity of every person;
- Justice, equity, and compassion in human relations;
- Acceptance of one another and encouragement to spiritual growth in our congregations;
- A free and responsible search for truth and meaning;
- The right of conscience and the use of the democratic process within our congregations and in society at large;
- The goal of world community with peace, liberty, and justice for all;
- Respect for the interdependent web of all existence of which we are a part.

The Six Sources

Unitarian Universalism draws from many sources.

- Direct experience of that transcending mystery and wonder, affirmed in all cultures, which moves us to a renewal of the spirit and an openness to the forces which create and uphold life;
- Words and deeds of prophetic women and men which challenge us to confront powers and structures of evil with justice, compassion, and the transforming power of love;
- Wisdom from the world's religions which inspires us in our ethical and spiritual life;
- Jewish and Christian teachings which call us to respond to God's love by loving our neighbors as ourselves;
- Humanist teachings which counsel us to heed the guidance of reason and the results of

science, and warn us against idolatries of the mind and spirit;

— Spiritual teachings of earth-centered traditions which celebrate the sacred circle of life and instruct us to live in harmony with the rhythms of nature.

All Are Welcome

Although many Unitarian Universalists were born in this faith, many more came to it later in life. Some of these seekers left the faith tradition of their childhood, while others came from no religious tradition at all. Interfaith families have frequently found a religious home in a Unitarian Universalist congregation, where each partner's beliefs and traditions are honored and children can learn about their parents' faith heritage and eventually seek their own answers to religious questions.

Our Unitarian heritage calls us to recognize the inherent good of all persons, while the Universalist part of our tradition encourages us to extend love and acceptance to all people. You are welcome in a Unitarian Universalist congregation, whatever your gender identity, sexual orientation, racial identity, or class. Our Principles call us to affirm the worth and dignity of every individual, to accept one another, and to foster each other's spiritual growth.

Congregational Covenant

A covenant is a promise that members of a congregation make to one another, transforming them from a collection of individuals into a faith community. Spoken in unison, the covenant is often part of the Sunday service. Congregations choose their own covenant statement. Here is one popular example.

Love is the doctrine of this church,
The quest of Truth is its sacrament,
And service is its prayer.
To dwell together in peace,
To seek knowledge in freedom,
To serve human need,
To the end that all souls shall
grow into harmony with the Divine—
Thus do we covenant with each other
    and with God.

Chalice Lightings

Worship begins with the lighting of the chalice and
the recitation of opening words. This simple ritual,
a combination of gesture and word, evokes within us
a spirit of reverence, shared community, and hope.

Glory be to the earth and the wind.
Glory be to the sun and the rain.
Glory be to animals and children
    and women and men.
Glory be to our holy flame
    which calls us together as one.

—BETTYE A. DOTY

I call that mind free which jealously guards its
intellectual rights and powers, which calls no one
master, which does not content itself with a pas-

sive or hereditary faith, which opens itself to light whencesoever it may come, which receives new truth as an angel from heaven.

—WILLIAM ELLERY CHANNING

Come into the circle of love and justice.
Come into the community of mercy, holiness,
    and health.
Come and you shall know peace and joy.

—ISRAEL ZANGWILL, ADAPTED

Life is a gift for which we are grateful.
We gather in community to celebrate the glories
    and the mysteries of this great gift.

—MARJORIE MONTGOMERY

We light this chalice for the light of truth.
We light this chalice for the warmth of love.
We light this chalice for the energy of action.

—MARY ANN MOORE

May the light of this chalice give light and
    warmth to our family,
On good days and bad, happy and sad,
And may we feel the warmth spread from our
    family circle
to wider and wider circles,
Until we feel our family part of the one circle
    of life.

—BETSY DARR

Worship Readings

We gather to share a sense of transcendence, to nurture worthiness and meaning in our lives. The act of worship reminds us of our capacity to heal, to change, and to belong.

O Spinner, Weaver, of our lives,
Your loom is love.
May we who are gathered here
be empowered by that love
to weave new patterns of Truth
and Justice into a web of life that is strong,
beautiful, and everlasting.

—BARBARA WELLS TEN HOVE

Spirit of life, be present with us this hour.
Join us today as we gather in a wider search for
    truth and purpose.

In this quest, may we greet one another
with open hearts and minds;
may we inspire each other to consider new
    questions
and seek deeper meaning;
may we cultivate wisdom and compassion.
Let all who enter this sanctuary see a welcome
    face,
hear a kind word, and
find comfort in this community.
And may all that is done and said here today
be in service to love and justice.

—KATHY HUFF

Why should we live in such a hurry and waste of
life?

*We are determined to be starved before we are
hungry.*

I wish to live deliberately, to front only the essen-
tial facts of life.

I wish to learn what life has to teach, and not, when I come to die, discover that I have not lived.

I do not wish to live what is not life, living is so dear,

Nor do I wish to practice resignation, unless it is quite necessary.

I wish to live deep and suck out all the marrow of life,

I want to cut a broad swath, to drive life into a corner, and reduce it to its lowest terms.

If it proves to be mean, then to get the whole and genuine meanness of it, and publish its meanness to the world;

Or if it is sublime, to know it by experience, and to be able to give a true account of it.

—HENRY DAVID THOREAU

In this familiar place, listen:
to the sounds of breathing, creaking chairs,
shuffling feet, clearing throats, and sighing all
    around
Know that each breath, movement, the glance
meant for you or intercepted
holds a life within it.

These are signs
that we choose to be in this company
have things to say to each other
things not yet said but in each other's presence
    still trembling behind our hearts' doors
these doors closed but unlocked
each silent thing waiting
on the threshold between unknowing and
    knowing,
between being hidden and being known.

Find the silence among these people
and listen to it all—breathing, sighs,
movement, holding back—
hear the tears that have not yet reached their eyes

perhaps they are your own
hear also the laughter building deep where joy
    abides
despite everything.
Listen: rejoice.   And say Amen.

—BARBARA PESCAN

With faith to face our challenges,
with love that casts out fear,
with hope to trust tomorrow,
we accept this day as the gift it is:
    a reason for rejoicing.

—GARY KOWALSKI

Be ours a religion which, like sunshine,
    goes everywhere;
its temple, all space;
its shrine, the good heart;
its creed, all truth;
its ritual, works of love;
its profession of faith, divine living.

—THEODORE PARKER

Amid all the noise in our lives,
we take this moment to sit in silence—
 to give thanks for another day,
 to give thanks for all those in our lives who
  have brought us warmth and love,
 to give thanks for the gift of life.

We know we are on our pilgrimage here but a
 brief moment in time.

Let us open ourselves, here, now,
to the process of becoming more whole—
 of living more fully,
 of giving and forgiving more freely,
 of understanding more completely the
  meaning of our lives here on this earth.

       —TIMOTHY HALEY

This house is for the ingathering of nature and
human nature.

*It is a house of friendships, a haven in trouble, an
open room for the encouragement of our struggle.*

It is a house of freedom, guarding the dignity and worth of every person.

It offers a platform for the free voice, for declaring, both in times of security and danger, the full and undivided conflict of opinion.

It is a house of truth-seeking, where scientists can encourage devotion to their quest, where mystics can abide in a community of searchers.

It is a house of art, adorning its celebrations with melodies and handiworks.

It is a house of prophecy, outrunning times past and times present in visions of growth and progress.

This house is a cradle for our dreams, the workshop of our common endeavor.

—KENNETH L. PATTON

To live content with small means;
To seek elegance rather than luxury, and
    refinement rather than fashion;

To be worthy, not respectable, and wealthy, not
   rich;
To study hard, think quietly, talk gently, act
   frankly;
To listen to stars and birds, to babes and sages,
   with open heart;
To bear all cheerfully, do all bravely, await
   occasions, hurry never.
To let the spiritual, unbidden and unconscious,
   grow up through the common.
This is to be my symphony.

—WILLIAM HENRY CHANNING

I am only one
But still I am one.
I cannot do everything,
But still I can do something.
And because I cannot do everything
I will not refuse to do the something that I can do.

—EDWARD EVERETT HALE

I am glad I came into this world able to think and reason.

I am glad I came into this world able to feel pain and pleasure, sorrow and joy, anger and love.

I am glad I am able to heal, both physically and mentally; able to be aware, to grow and to change.

I am glad I am able to respond to love, beauty and truth: able to discern reality, face it, accept it.

I am glad I came into this world able to feel with others, to care for others.

I am glad I came into this world unique and singular.

I am glad I came into this world as an unfinished creature, moving towards completion.

I give thanks for the many gifts of life.
I am glad I came into this world.

—MARJORIE MONTGOMERY

May the light around us guide our footsteps,
and hold us fast to the best and most righteous
that we seek.

May the darkness around us nurture our
dreams,
and give us rest so that we may give ourselves to
the work of our world.

Let us seek to remember the wholeness of our
lives,
the weaving of light and shadow in this great
and astonishing dance in which we move.

—KATHLEEN MCTIGUE

We receive fragments of holiness, glimpses of eternity, brief moments of insight. Let us gather them up for the precious gifts that they are and, renewed by their grace, move boldly into the unknown.

—SARA YORK

For the sun and the dawn
Which we did not create;

For the moon and the evening
Which we did not make;

For food which we plant
But cannot grow;

For friends and loved ones
We have not earned and cannot buy;

For this gathered company
Which welcomes us as we are,
from wherever we have come;

For all our free churches
That keep us human and encourage us in our
quest for beauty, truth, and love;

For all things which come to us
As gifts of being from sources beyond ourselves;

Gifts of life and love and friendship
We lift up our hearts in thanks this day.

—RICHARD M. FEWKES

If, recognizing the interdependence of all life,
we strive to build community,
the strength we gather will be our salvation.

If you are black and I am white,

It will not matter.

If you are female and I am male,

It will not matter.

If you are older and I am younger,

It will not matter.

If you are progressive and I am conservative,

It will not matter.

If you are straight and I am gay,

It will not matter.

If you are Christian and I am Jewish,

It will not matter.

If we join spirits as brothers and sisters, the pain of our aloneness will be lessened, and that does matter.

In this spirit, we build community and move toward restoration.

—MARJORIE BOWENS-WHEATLEY

Cherish your doubts, for doubt is the servant of
   truth.
Question your convictions, for beliefs too
   tightly held strangle the mind and its natural
   wisdom.
Suspect all certitudes, for the world whirls on—
   nothing abides.
Yet in our inner rooms full of doubt, inquiry and
   suspicion, let a corner be reserved for trust.
For without trust there is no space for communities to gather or for friendships to be forged.
Indeed, this is the small corner where we
   connect—and reconnect—with each other.

—MICHAEL A. SCHULER

For the expanding grandeur of Creation, worlds known and unknown, galaxies beyond galaxies, filling us with awe and challenging our imaginations:

We give thanks this day.

For this fragile planet earth, its times and tides, its sunsets and seasons:

We give thanks this day.

For the joy of human life, its wonders and surprises, its hopes and achievements:

We give thanks this day.

For our human community, our common past and future hope, our oneness transcending all separation, our capacity to work for peace and justice in the midst of hostility and oppression:

We give thanks this day.

For high hopes and noble causes, for faith without fanaticism, for understanding of views not shared:

We give thanks this day.

For all who have labored and suffered for a fairer world, who have lived so that others might live in dignity and freedom:

We give thanks this day.

For human liberty and sacred rites; for opportunities to change and grow, to affirm and choose:

We give thanks this day. We pray that we may live not by our fears but by our hopes, not by our words but by our deeds.

—O. Eugene Pickett

In the end it won't matter how much we have,
but how generously we have given.
It won't matter how much we know,
but rather how well we live.
And it won't matter how much we believe,
but how deeply we love.

—John Morgan

Eternal Spirit, whom we call God,
   you are our life.
You are the best and the most beautiful in us and
      beyond us.
Your spirit is in animals, birds, plants, and in
      people
   whom we do not know or who seem very
      different from us.
All of us share the gift of life.
Help us to remember that life is good.
Help us to know that we don't stop loving people
      or other living
   things when they are no longer close to us.
Love lasts always.
May we look for ways to love one another, and
      to love
   all living things. Amen.

—Lucinda Steven Duncan

We have a calling in this world:
we are called to honor diversity,

to respect differences with dignity,
and to challenge those who would forbid it.
We are people of a wide path.
Let us be wide in affection
and go our way in peace.

—Jean M. Rowe

Universal Spirit of love,
O God within each one of us,
whose power reaches to the stars,
whose love connects us one to another
and to all creation—we are one.

—Dorothy May Emerson

The years of all of us are short, our lives precarious.

Our days and nights go hurrying on and there is
scarcely time to do the little that we might.

Yet we find time for bitterness, for petty treason and
evasion.

What can we do to stretch our hearts enough to lose their littleness?

Here we are—all of us—all upon this planet, bound together in a common destiny,

Living our lives between the briefness of the daylight and the dark.

Kindred in this, each lighted by the same precarious, flickering flame of life, how does it happen that we are not kindred in all things else?

How strange and foolish are these walls of separation that divide us!

—A. POWELL DAVIES

These are the days that have been given to us;
let us rejoice and be glad in them.
These are the days of our lives;
let us live them well in love and service.
These are the days of mystery and wonder;
let us cherish and celebrate them in gratitude
    together.

These are the days that have been given to us;
let us make of them stories worth telling to those
who come after us.

—WILLIAM R. MURRY

Holy and beautiful the custom which brings us
together,
In the presence of the Most High:

To face our ideals,
To remember our loved ones in absence,
To give thanks, to make confession,
To offer forgiveness,
To be enlightened, and to be strengthened.

Through this quiet hour breathes
The worship of ages,
The cathedral music of history.

Three unseen guests attend,
Faith, hope, and love:
Let all our hearts prepare them place.

—ROBERT FRENCH LEAVENS

If, here, you have found freedom,
take it with you into the world.

If you have found comfort,
go and share it with others.

If you have dreamed dreams,
help one another,
that they may come true!

If you have known love,
give some back
to a bruised and hurting world.

Go in peace.

—LAURALYN BELLAMY

Let us go forth into the world
through a door of hope for the future,
remembering these words by Martin Luther:
Even if I knew that tomorrow
the world would go to pieces,
I would still plant my apple tree.

—MARJORIE NEWLIN LEAMING

Go in peace. Live simply, gently, at home in
    yourselves.
Act justly.
Speak justly.
Remember the depth of your own compassion.
Forget not your power in the days of your
    powerlessness.

Do not desire to be wealthier than your peers
and stint not your hand of charity.
Practice forbearance.
Speak the truth, or speak not.
Take care of yourselves as bodies, for you are a
    good gift.

Crave peace for all people in the world,
beginning with yourselves,
and go as you go with the dream of that peace
    alive in your heart.

—MARK BELLETINI

Spirit of Life

Spir - it of Life, come un - to me.

Sing in my heart all the stir - rings of com - pas - sion.

Blow in the wind, rise in the sea;

move in the hand, giv - ing life the shape of jus - tice.

Roots hold me close; wings set me free;

Spir - it of Life, come to me, come to me.

Words and music by Carolyn McDade

We Gather Together

1. We gath - er to - geth - er in joy - ful thanks - giv - ing, ac - claim - ing cre - a - tion, whose boun - ty we share; both sor - row and glad - ness we find now in our liv - ing, we sing a hymn of praise to the life that we bear.

2. We gath - er to - geth - er to join in the jour - ney, con - firm - ing, com - mit - ting our pas - sage to be a true af - fir - ma - tion, in joy and trib - u - la - tion, when bound to hu - man care and hope– then we are free.

Words by Dorothy Caiger Senghas and Robert Senghas

Religious Education

Unitarian Universalists believe that education is an inherent aspect of spiritual growth. Our religious education programming addresses the needs of people throughout the life span, providing opportunities for children, youth, and adults to engage their minds as a way to grow their hearts. Religious education helps us understand that divine inspiration can be found within each human being, that we are born with the potential for goodness, that salvation is available to all, and that we have a duty to cherish the earth and revere life.

Parents seek religious education programs that are based in a community of shared values. These values provide children with building blocks to help them form their own beliefs. We have a strong faith in the inherent spirituality of children and see it as our task to nurture that spirit. Our respect for children teaches them also to have respect—

for themselves, for others, and for the fragile inter-dependent web of all life.

We begin with the understanding that children, like adults, learn in different ways. They engage their bodies, spirits, imaginations, and curiosity as part of their religious learning. Stories, discussion, games, art projects, and music are just some of the ways we help children explore their world and gain new knowledge and insights.

We teach children that all big questions have many answers, and that it is their duty to search responsibly for the answers that feel right to them. Children learn that there are as many ideas about God as there are people; that we consider Jesus to be one of the great prophets and teachers and learn from the example of his life; and that death is a mystery inseparable from life, and the only immortality we can know for sure is the way we live on in the hearts and minds of those whose lives we touch. Therefore, how we lead our lives each day is of utmost importance.

Our religious education programs teach our Unitarian Universalist heritage. Children learn about Unitarian and Universalist forebears such as John Adams, second president of the United States; Susan B. Anthony, who worked for women's rights; Alexander Graham Bell, who invented the telephone; and Clara Barton, founder of the American Red Cross.

Our children learn about the Bible in age-appropriate ways. Though we do not teach it as the literal word of God, the Bible is important to us for at least three reasons: first, we find in it good lessons and inspiring words; second, it helps us understand our Western cultural heritage; and third, knowing about the Bible from a historical perspective helps children explain their own beliefs to others who are biblically oriented.

Children also learn about the beliefs and practices of the world's major religions. This encourages understanding of other cultures, fosters the sense of being a world citizen, and helps children see our Jewish and Christian cultures in perspective.

Finally, religious education teaches children about ethical living. They learn about the moral precepts to love your neighbor, to work for a better world, and to search for truth with an open mind.

To find out about programs for children, youth, young adults, and adults, check your congregation's bulletin board. The church newsletter and website are also good sources of information.

Social Justice

Unitarian Universalism offers a spiritual foundation and a supportive community for those who make social action part of their lives. Our congregations seek to build bridges from the individual to the wider society by using their collective voices and power. The preciousness of life on earth, the inherent worth and dignity of every person, and our mutual interdependency emerge as common themes for undertaking social justice work. The seven Principles of Unitarian Universalism are infused with this commitment.

Throughout Unitarian and Universalist history, women and men have shown great courage and taken huge personal risks on behalf of their vision of a better world. Famous American Unitarians and Universalists, such as suffragist Susan B. Anthony, civil rights leader Whitney Young, diplomat Adlai Stevenson, and American Red Cross founder Clara

Barton, are joined by thousands of Unitarian Universalists of lesser renown who have spent decades laboring for justice in their own communities.

Unitarian Universalism offers a spiritual home where people can find affirmation, encouragement, and inspiration for the slow and often difficult work of making justice. Members of a congregation often work together on social action projects, pooling their efforts to do good in the world.

Environmental activism is an integral part of social justice work. Our seventh Principle, affirming the interdependent web of all existence, provides a spiritual sensibility that binds us with all living creatures and inspires social and political action on behalf of our planet.

The Story of Unitarian Universalism

The roots of Unitarianism and Universalism reach back to the dawning years of the Christian church. Some early Christians believed that God was a single entity and that Jesus, while a messenger of God, was fully human. In the year 325 these unitarian ideas were declared heresy when the Council of Nicea established the doctrine of the Trinity. The universalist doctrine that all will be saved was taught by early church fathers such as Origen and Clement of Alexandria. The idea of universal salvation was rejected by an ecumenical council in 553.

In the sixteenth century, in the spirit of the Reformation in Europe, many began to challenge the official doctrine of the church on these questions. Michael Servetus was burned at the stake in Geneva for arguing against the Trinity. Francis

David introduced Unitarian ideas to Transylvania, where the Unitarian church endured despite persecution and survives to this day.

Unitarian ideas appeared in Holland and England, where influential figures such as John Milton and Isaac Newton privately adopted the forbidden theology. Illegal churches sprang up but were soon suppressed. In the late eighteenth century, the English chemist and preacher Joseph Priestley, whose home had been burned by a mob, moved to Pennsylvania and in 1794 started the first American church founded as Unitarian.

Universalist ideas also took root in America in the second half of the eighteenth century, as charismatic preachers spread the faith throughout the Northeast. Most notably, John Murray, a Methodist preacher; Dr. George de Benneville, a physician and lay preacher; and Caleb Rich, a Baptist minister, preached about God's love redeeming us all. In 1780 Murray founded the first Universalist church in America in Gloucester, Massachusetts. Other Universalist congregations soon sprang up.

During the emerging American revolution, many Massachusetts ministers began to turn toward unitarianism. By the early 1800s tension was building between the liberals and those with more traditional views. In 1819 the disagreement culminated in William Ellery Channing's famous sermon "Unitarian Christianity," which asserted the Unitarian doctrine. The American Unitarian Association was founded in 1825.

The first half of the nineteenth century also saw the rise of a second generation of Universalist preachers, led by Hosea Ballou. He combined a unitarian vision with his universalism. Under Ballou's influence, the idea of the Trinity disappeared from Universalist theology. Spreading throughout the Midwest and upper South, Universalists took up social reform as a response to the call to model God's love on earth.

By the 1840s a new religious current had developed within Unitarianism—Transcendentalism. The Transcendentalists believed in the individual's direct experience with the divine, unity with nature, and a religious duty to provide prophetic witness to the social issues of the day. Ralph Waldo Emerson and Theodore Parker were the two most prominent shapers of these controversial ideas.

A number of prominent writers and thinkers of the nineteenth century were Unitarian, including Henry David Thoreau, Oliver Wendell Holmes, Henry Wadsworth Longfellow and his cousin Samuel Longfellow, William Cullen Bryant, Louisa May Alcott, George Bancroft, Margaret Fuller, and Francis Parkman.

Both Unitarians and Universalists were well represented among prominent abolitionists, supporters of women's rights, and other leaders for social reform. These included Horace Mann, father of public education; mental health reformer Dorothea Dix; the abolitionists John Quincy Adams, Samuel May, and Julia Ward Howe; and the women's rights leaders Susan B. Anthony, Olympia Brown, Mary Livermore, and Elizabeth Cady Stanton.

After the Civil War the two religious traditions gradually evolved on parallel paths. Both embraced the theory of evolution. Both perceived scientific achievement as a confirmation of the steady advancement of humanity toward moral and material perfection and saw social reform as a means toward this perfection.

Some ministers from both traditions began to advocate a new post-Christian theology, and some rejected belief in a supernatural God altogether. For the Unitarians, the twentieth century saw the rise of humanism, which placed the responsibility for human welfare solely in human hands. Though the Universalists remained predominantly Christian, they became open to other paths to truth and insights from the world's religions.

During World War II the Unitarians founded the Unitarian Service Committee to aid European refugees escaping from Nazism. After the war the Service Committee expanded its mission throughout the world. The Universalists created their own Service Committee on the Unitarian model, and the two agencies frequently cooperated on projects. Both Unitarians and Universalists became strong advocates for establishing the United Nations.

•　•　•

After decades of cooperation in areas of worship, religious education, and youth activities, the two traditions combined in 1961 to form the Unitarian Universalist Association (known as the UUA). The decades that followed, times of deep social change in America, brought new challenges and triumphs.

The UUA was not quite four years old when Rev. Dr. Martin Luther King Jr. sent an urgent telegram to its Boston headquarters, asking religious leaders and concerned citizens to join him in Selma, Alabama, where African Americans marching for their right to vote had been brutally attacked by police. Two of the Unitarian Universalists who responded to King's appeal paid with their lives. The murders of the Rev. James Reeb and Viola Gregg Liuzzo galvanized the nation. In all, about 500 Unitarian Universalists went to Selma and Montgomery to participate in the civil rights campaign.

Many African Americans had been attracted to Unitarian Universalism because of its involvement in civil rights. However, a funding controversy about how to empower African Americans within

Unitarian Universalism rocked the UUA in the late 1960s, causing many to become disillusioned and leave in bitterness.

In the aftermath of the controversy, Unitarian Universalists turned their attention increasingly to racial reconciliation and cultural diversity, building up to a watershed resolution passed by the General Assembly in 1997. Titled "Toward an Anti-Racist Unitarian Universalist Association," this resolution marked the beginning of a multi-faceted commitment to engage more deeply in the struggle for racial justice. These efforts have become an accepted and inspiring dimension in Unitarian Universalist institutional life.

The role of women has also changed. Both Unitarianism and Universalism had been early leaders in support of women's rights and were among the first denominations to ordain women ministers, but in 1970 only a small fraction of UU ministers were female. Women in positions of lay leadership began to demand change. They pressed successfully for equal opportunities in ministry and for gender-inclusive language in all dimensions of church life.

Gradually they transformed Unitarian Universalism. The leadership of women, both lay and clergy, was critical to the 1985 adoption of the Principles and Purposes. In 2000 the UUA became the first denomination in the United States to have women comprise more than 50 percent of its active clergy.

In 1970, the UUA General Assembly passed its first general resolution affirming support for bisexual, gay, and lesbian people in their struggle for equal rights and acceptance. The UUA Office of Gay Concerns, established in 1974, is now the Office of Bisexual, Gay, Lesbian, and Transgender Concerns. The UUA has officially supported its clergy who perform services of union between same-sex couples since 1984, and in 1996 it was the first mainline denomination in the country to support legalized same-sex marriage.

During these years, Unitarian Universalism became more welcoming of diverse theological perspectives. A new ecological awareness inspired not only social and political action but also a deepening spirituality. Worship flourished as a result of the rich influences of Buddhism, earth-centered traditions, and Native American spirituality. Earth-centered spirituality is now an acknowledged source of inspiration for Unitarian Universalists, alongside Jewish and Christian teachings, the wisdom of other world religions, humanism, prophetic witness, and direct experience of the transcendent mysteries of life.

A Unitarian Universalist congregation today is likely to include members whose positions on faith are derived from a variety of religious beliefs: Jewish, Christian, Buddhist, Pagan, atheist, or agnostic. We might call ourselves religious humanists, liberal Christians, or world religionists, but we are all faithful Unitarian Universalists committed to the practice of free religion.

Unitarian Universalism entered the new century with a history that stretches back to the early years of Christianity, yet the UUA is less than fifty years old as an organization. Our story is constantly changing, evolving, and unfolding. We are urged on by our love for one another and for the divine. Our future is as unlimited as our quest.

Quotable Quotes

Language has the power to inspire us—to call us to action and to navigate the delicate path between ourselves as individuals and as members of a community. On these pages are the words of Unitarian Universalists and their forebears on matters of faith, spirituality, good works, and more.

We stand in a tradition of abundance. We have said for centuries that there is room in our religion for every kind of seeker and sojourner. We are called to embody a generosity of spirit, an open and optimistic view of God and of life, that claims that everyone is included. Skeptics and poets and scientists are welcome here, as are nonconformists and shy and uncertain folk, and all manner of smart people and foolish ones. I believe that our restlessness and doubts have a divine origin and are a sign of grace. Our love of truth can be understood as the holiest of gifts. Our devotion to truth may be the means of our deliverance.

—BARBARA MERRITT, *minister*

A living tradition is not bequeathed through some law of inheritance; it must be earned, not without dust and heat, and not without humbling grace.

—JAMES LUTHER ADAMS (1901–1994), *minister*

Ultimately, we are all theologians. We all ponder the great life issues. As Unitarian Universalists we celebrate common operational values that unite us even as we enjoy a diversity of perspectives that enables us to learn and grow religiously.

—RICHARD GILBERT, *minister*

Most of the great Western theologians agree at least on this: God is beyond naming or full understanding, yet we human beings, created in God's image, nonetheless are called to make the attempt.

It is the free faith of Unitarian Universalism that makes my attempts worthwhile.

—Rosemary Bray-McNatt, *minister*

Religious education is far more than classroom teaching of subject matter. It is also far more than an opportunity for a polemical presentation of one theological or social point of view. Religious education must be for all members of congregations. It takes place at board meetings, in meetings of the worship committee, on retreats, in adult classes, and when children are present with adults in Sunday services.

—Spencer Lavan, *minister*

The word freedom comes from an ancient Norse root verb that means to become loving. Freedom is not properly a state of being then, but more accurately a choice for becoming. So, in our religion, freedom is about becoming, never about being.

—Terry Sweetser, *minister*

All people and cultures without exception hold myths to be true. Anyone who believes that others —less sophisticated—may naïvely hold myths to be true while they themselves do not, are themselves naïve.

—ALICE BLAIR WESLEY, *minister*

The critical way is the way of those who believe the certainty offered by the religions is unobtainable by anyone. We believe that ultimate questions must of necessity have open-ended answers.

—DUNCAN HOWLETT (1906–2003), *minister*

The Bible is holy scripture because it is a living document and foundation of many important faiths, including Unitarian Universalism. To abandon the Bible would mean alienation from one of the world's most important influences on religious thought—liberal and otherwise. Our UU Principles and Purposes are saturated with biblical concepts and ideals. Our concept of respect for the web of existence, for instance, emanates from a stream of thought that flows through the Psalms and the Prophets from that same God of Genesis who declared the goodness of creation.

—DAVID MCFARLAND, *minister*

Humanism teaches that our well-being and our very existence depend upon the web of life in ways we are only beginning to understand, that our place in nature has to be in harmony with it. Humanism leads me to find a sense of wider relatedness with all the world and its peoples, and it calls me to work for a sound environment and a humane civilization. Because everything is interconnected, I cannot be concerned with my own life and the future of humanity without also being concerned about the future of the planet.

—SARAH OELBERG, *minister*

The language of reverence is, finally, the language of humanity. The human experience of finding ourselves in the presence of that intense, fleeting, and demanding moment when the dull surfaces of things become transparent to a significance almost greater than we can bear belongs to all of us.

—KENDYL GIBBONS, *minister*

I like to think of mysticism as the art of meeting reality, or the art of richer and deeper awareness, for it seems to me that union with reality can hardly be consciously cultivated. It is an experience that comes unbidden, but which may come more often as we go out to meet persons and the world, and as we are more sensitively, more richly, more profoundly aware. . . . There are moments when life seems vivid and resplendent, when a more than mortal splendor breaks in, when there is a touch of grandeur and of glory in just being alive.

—JACOB TRAPP (1899–1992), *minister*

Each night a child is born is a holy night.

—SOPHIA LYON FAHS (1876–1978),
religious educator

To me, human life in all its forms, individual and aggregate, is a perpetual wonder; the Flora of the earth and sea is full of beauty and of mystery which science seeks to understand; the fauna of land and ocean is not less wonderful; the world which holds them both, and the great universe that folds it in on every side, are still more wonderful, complex, and attractive, to the contemplating mind.

—THEODORE PARKER (1810–1860), *minister*

I would like to believe when I die that I have given myself away like a tree that sows seeds every spring and never counts the loss, because it is not loss, it is adding to future life. It is the tree's way of being. Strongly rooted, perhaps, but spilling out its treasure on the wind.

—MAY SARTON (1912–1995), *poet*

Unitarian Universalism is faith in people, hope for tomorrow's child, confidence in a continuity that spans all time. It looks not to a perfect heaven, but toward a good earth. It is respectful of the past, but

not limited to it. It is trust in growing and con-
spiracy with change. It is spiritual responsibility
for a moral tomorrow.

—ED SCHEMPP (1908–2003), *activist*

Our religion is a religion of social concern, a religion of intellectual and ethical integrity, a religion
that emphasizes the dynamic conception of history and the scientific worldview, a religion that
stresses the dignity and worth of the person as a
supreme value and goodwill as the creative force
in human relations. This religion can and ought to
become a beacon from which this kind of faith
shines.

—LEWIS A. MCGEE (1893–1979), *minister*

If in our time the faith of some seems to falter, if
today we may be less sure of success, if now we
seem less certain that the old promises will be ful-
filled, we yet must continue. All of us know how
dark and dangerous is this time in human history—
no one would deny it. Perhaps the very density of

the darkness will cause more persons to kindle lights. We must continue to work for world community. Because we are who we are, we can do no other.

—ROBERT WEST, *minister*

If a theology of liberation suggests human transformation through active participation and "active agency" in one's life, it must also point to having what one needs to physically live and to achieve fulfillment as a human being.

—PATRICIA JIMENEZ, *minister*

True religion, like our founding principles, requires that the rights of the disbeliever be equally acknowledged with those of the believer.

—A. POWELL DAVIES (1902–1957), *minister*

This is what we do with our faith. Live in this world knowing that we will lose each other, loving despite the hard bargain it makes of us. Do what we can to make the world a place where this truth can be safely lived, measuring our faith by the difference we have made. Build faith communities to continue after we are gone, where we are remembered by lives of good works and care; worlds we have made so that others might live.

—JUDITH MEYER, *minister*

We are a gentle and generous people. But let us not forget our anger. May it fuel not only our commitment to compassion but also our commitment to make fundamental changes. Our vision of the Beloved Community must stand against a vision that would allow the privilege of the few to be accepted as just and even holy. Our religious vision must again and again ask the Gospel question "Who is my neighbor" and strive always to include more and more of us as we intone the words that gave birth to this nation, "We the people. . . ." We are, and we should be, both a gentle, and an angry people.

—WILLIAM SINKFORD, *minister*

If one fights relentlessly against injustice, want, hate, and every form of exploitation, then one is a religious person. The love of God is not expressed by ritual or ceremony, but by loving.

—WADE H. McCREE, JR. (1920–1987),
U.S. judge

Liberal theology is not for the faint of heart. It points us in a general direction without telling us the specific destination. It refuses to make our commitments for us, but holds us accountable to the commitments we make. . . . It invites us to live with ambiguity without giving in to facile compromise; to engage in dialogue without trying to control the conversation; to be open to change without accepting change too casually; to take commitment seriously but not blindly; to be engaged in the culture without succumbing to the culture's values.

—PAUL RASOR, *minister*

Religion is our human response to the dual reality of being alive and having to die.

—Forrest Church, *minister*

Perhaps we should realize that our need is not to "find something to believe"—but rather to discover that our lives indicate what we believe right now. This is the place to start.

—Edith Hunter, *religious educator*

Stand by this faith. Work for it and sacrifice for it. There is nothing in all the world so important as to be loyal to this faith which has placed before us the loftiest ideals, which has comforted us in sorrow, strengthened us for noble duty and made the world beautiful.

—Olympia Brown (1835–1926), *minister*

The miracle of Exodus is not whether or not the Red Sea parted. That is nothing more than a poetic conceit. The miracle of Exodus is that a group of people finally realized for themselves, for us, and for all time that you cannot stay in Egypt. Any personal commitment that is not toward growing and changing, any religious commitment that is not toward goals beyond one's own personal welfare, is a commitment toward slavery in Egypt.

—JOHN HAYS NICHOLS, *minister*

We have to "leave home," in a sense, leave our comfortable ways of being, to find ourselves and our calling. We need to develop a passionate discontent, an anger that picks us up and shakes us by the neck and will not let us go. The Holy Spirit, you know, is not on the side of order and stability.

—MARILYN SEWELL, *minister*

The Beloved Community is not an organization of individuals seeking private and selfish security for their souls. It is a new adventure, a spontaneous fellowship of consecrated men seeking a new world.

—CLARENCE SKINNER (1881–1949), *minister*

We need to love from the start—not as an emergency strategy when everything has gone wrong. We need to love our neighbors as ourselves through economic systems that pay a living wage for labor instead of indulging in policies that allow the rich to get richer and the poor to be left behind when the storm comes. We need to love the world through reverence that fosters observant attention to the intricate relationality of life.

—REBECCA PARKER, *minister*

The renaissance for human dignity is moving forward, helping not only the oppressed but also the oppressor to find the God within.

—EUGENE SPARROW (1921–1978), *minister*

Worship invites us to focus on the transcendental, the intimate, and the worthy. Worship helps us to regain our grip on the fragmented, the obsessive, and the divisive. Worship reminds us that we— empowered by the love we receive and give—may challenge any idol of greed or violence which pollutes the human condition. We ask that you bring to worship something of what you receive: a capacity to heal, to think both critically and poetically, and to experience a growing sense of belonging, rootedness, and blessing.

—MARK BELLETINI, *minister*

So if someone tells you that she or he knows pain, loneliness, loss, fear, and dismay, but does not know the feeling of being sustained by a love that is wider, deeper, and infinitely vaster than the sorrows, hear those words as a commission. Hear your commission to love, to create community, and to heal. One at a time in personal relationships, ten at a time in covenant groups, hundreds at a time in our congregations, hundreds of thousands at a time in our religious movement, millions at a time as we take our commission deeper and deeper into humanity's heart as a justice-loving people who will transform the world. This is the Good News of our faith.

—THANDEKA, *minister*

We affirm that every one of us is held in Creation's hand—a part of the interdependent cosmic web—and hence strangers need not be enemies; that no one is saved until we All are saved where All means the whole of Creation.

—WILLIAM SCHULZ, *minister*

Evil is the capacity, within us and among us, to break sacred bonds with our own souls, with one another, and with the holy. Further, it is the willingness to excuse or justify this damage, to deny it, or to call it virtue. The soil in which it flourishes is a rich compost of ignorance, arrogance, fear, and delusion—mostly self-delusion—all mingled with the sparkling dust of our original, human being.

—VICTORIA SAFFORD, *minister*

Blessed are you who know that the work of the church is transformation of society, who have a vision of Beloved Community transcending the present, and who do not shrink from controversy, sacrifice, or change. Blessed are you indeed.

—JOHN BUEHRENS, *minister*

We cannot more efficiently labor for the good of all men than by pledging heart, brain, and hands to the service of keeping our country true to its mission, obedient to its idea. . . . The world waits to see the quality and energy of our patriotism. The book of our country's history, preserved by human heroism and providential care, is handed to us, that we may inscribe there the records of its glory, or its shame.

—THOMAS STARR KING (1824–1864), *minister*

We are here dedicated to the proposition that beneath all our differences, behind all our diversity, there is a unity that makes us one and binds us forever together, in spite of time and death and the space between the stars. We pause in silent witness to that unity.

—DAVID BUMBAUGH, *minister*

Glossary

BRIDGING CEREMONY: The ritual that recognizes and celebrates our youth in their transition to young adulthood.

CHILD DEDICATION: A celebration of the blessing of new life, an expression of the parents' hopes for their child, and a call to the parents and members of the congregation to nurture the child's spiritual life.

CHURCH OF THE LARGER FELLOWSHIP (CLF): This Unitarian Universalist congregation has no church building. Instead, it exists on the Internet and in print, reaching out to those who are not members of a local congregation or who wish to connect to UUs around the world. CLF provides its members with worship materials, the newsletter *Quest*, the quarterly children's publication *UU & Me!*, and many online resources on religious education and other topics.

COMING OF AGE: A program in which youth, ages 12–14, meet to explore their spirituality and faith. Participants usually learn about Unitarian Universalism, develop their own belief statements (often called credos), and visit other UU congregations and the UUA headquarters in Boston. The equivalent of confirmation in the Christian tradition.

CONGREGATIONAL POLITY: The Unitarian Universalist system of governance. UU congregations call their own ministers and are self-governing, with authority and responsibility vested in their membership.

FLAMING CHALICE: Unitarian Universalist worship often begins with lighting the chalice. The chalice and the flame were brought together as a symbol by the Unitarian Service Committee in Portugal in 1941. The flaming chalice appeared in a seal for papers and a badge for agents moving refugees to freedom. In time it became a symbol for Unitarian Universalism all around the world.

FLOWER COMMUNION: A special worship service created by Norbert Fabián Čapek in Prague. Each member of the congregation brings a flower to the service, and worship begins with members placing the flowers in a basket. At the close of the service, each member takes another flower from the collective basket. Introduced to the United States in the spring of 1940, the Flower Communion is now widely celebrated by Unitarian Universalist congregations. Many follow the tradition of making this the last service of the church year before the summer begins.

GENERAL ASSEMBLY: The annual business meeting of the UUA, attended by delegates from UU congregations and others who are interested in the General Assembly's workshops, worship services, and opportunities for fellowship.

GREEN SANCTUARY: A UUA program that helps congregations develop an awareness of environmental issues, encourage personal lifestyle changes, and work to address environmental injustices.

HUMANISM: A philosophy that stresses the human aspect of life here and now and puts the responsibility for ethical behavior upon each individual. Humanism also focuses on rational rather than supernatural religious explanations. Modern-day religious humanism is largely derived from the writings of early American Unitarian humanists, including Joseph Priestley, Thomas Jefferson, and John Haynes Holmes. Almost half of Unitarian Universalists today define themselves as humanists.

INTERDEPENDENT WEB: This metaphor conveys the philosophical idea, confirmed by science, that all living things exist in dependence upon one another. Found in the phrase "the interdependent web of all existence," from the seventh Principle of Unitarian Universalism, adopted by the General Assembly in 1985.

OUR WHOLE LIVES (OWL): A series of multi-age sexuality education curricula published by the

UUA and the United Church of Christ for use in both secular and religious settings. In UU settings, these curricula are used with their companion curricula, *Sexuality and Our Faith*.

SINGING THE LIVING TRADITION: UUA hymnbook, published in 1993. In addition to 415 hymns, *Singing the Living Tradition* includes more than 300 readings from diverse religious and cultural sources.

SINGING THE JOURNEY: Supplement to the UUA hymnal, *Singing the Living Tradition*. Features 75 selections, including jazz, folk, pop, spirituals, gospel, praise songs, call-and-response songs, chants, rounds, and traditional hymns. Published in 2005.

TAPESTRY OF FAITH: Online religious education programs and resources for all ages. Designed to nurture Unitarian Universalist identity, spiritual growth, a transforming faith, and vital communities of justice and love, Tapestry of Faith resources are downloadable, printable, viewable, and interactive—a religious growth and learning program for the twenty-first century. This resource is still in development. To find it online, go to www.uua. org/tapestryoffaith.

TRANSCENDENTALISM: A movement in literature, religion, culture, and philosophy that emerged in New England in the early to middle nineteenth century. Among Transcendentalists' core beliefs was an ideal spiritual state that transcends the physical and empirical and is realized through personal intuition rather than the doctrines of established religion. Prominent Transcendentalists included Ralph Waldo Emerson, Henry David Thoreau, Margaret Fuller, Bronson Alcott, Orestes Brownson, Frederick Henry Hedge, Theodore Parker, George Putnam, Elizabeth Peabody, and Sophia Peabody, wife of Nathaniel Hawthorne.

UU WORLD: The quarterly magazine of the Unitarian Universalist Association published for members of UUA congregations.

WELCOMING CONGREGATION: A program for Unitarian Universalist congregations that want to become more welcoming to bisexual, gay, lesbian, and/or transgender people. Developed by the UUA, the program consists of a series of workshops aimed at reducing prejudice by increasing understanding and acceptance among people of different sexual orientations.

Resources

Brandenburg, Ellen, ed. *The Seven Principles in Word and Worship.* Boston: Skinner House, 2007.

Buehrens, John A., and Forrest Church. *A Chosen Faith: An Introduction to Unitarian Universalism.* Revised ed. Boston: Beacon Press, 1998.

Dant, Jennifer. *Unitarian Universalism Is a Really Long Name.* Boston: Skinner House, 2006. (For children.)

Frost, Edward A., ed. *With Purpose and Principle: Essays About the Seven Principles of Unitarian Universalism.* Boston: Skinner House, 1998.

Grohsmeyer, Janeen. *A Lamp in Every Corner: Our Unitarian Universalist Storybook.* Boston: Unitarian Universalist Association, 2004.

Mendelsohn, Jack. *Being Liberal in an Illiberal Age: Why I Am a Unitarian Universalist.* 2nd ed. Boston: Skinner House, 2006.

Robinson, David. *The Unitarians and the Universalists.* Westport, Connecticut: Greenwood Press, 1985.

Sinkford, William. *Unitarian Universalist Pocket Guide.* 4th ed. Boston: Skinner House, 2004.

To learn more about Unitarian Universalism or to locate a congregation near you, please write to the Unitarian Universalist Association, or visit the Unitarian Universalist Association website. We welcome you to join us as we strive to work and worship together with respect, openness, and understanding.

Unitarian Universalist Association
25 Beacon Street
Boston, MA 02108-2800
(617) 742-2100

www.uua.org